"Welcome to 'Adventures in the Enchanted Garden'! Join us as we embark on a magical journey through lush greenery, colorful blooms, and secret wonders. In this enchanting garden, every corner holds a new discovery and every flower whispers a tale of wonder. Let your imagination bloom as we explore the mysteries and magic hidden within these hallowed grounds. Are you ready for an adventure like no other? Let's dive into the enchantment of the garden together!"

Made in the USA
Columbia, SC
30 March 2025

55873218R00046